Potty Train

In A Weekend

Mom of Four shares the secret to having your child potty trained in one weekend!

Becky Mansfield

OTHER BOOKS FROM
BECKY MANSFIELD

• • •

POTTY TRAIN IN A WEEKEND

Mom of four shares the secret to having your
child potty trained in a weekend.

Becky Mansfield

ISBN: 1496106334
ISBN 13: 9781496106339

This book is dedicated to my wonderful family. I am so grateful and thankful to have you in my life.

I want to thank all of the parents out there who have the love and passion, as a parent, to wake up each day and teach their child… keep doing an amazing job!

Table of contents

Meet The Author

Hi! I'm Becky, founder of the blog,
Your Modern Family.

Yourmodernfamily.com is dedicated to helping other parents raise their kids in the modern world, without stress. I share fun ideas and teaching tools to incorporate learning into play, as well as tips about how to organize your home through it all.

I am also the founder of Blogging on the Side, which teaches others how to blog, make money blogging and keep it on the side of more important things in life.

Outside of work, I am blessed to be the mother to four children and the wife to my high-school and college sweetheart.

Before our oldest son was born, I was an elementary teacher. Now that we have children, I am a part-time play therapist and stay at home mom. Working with young children has become second nature for me as I am able to study children, through play, on a daily basis. I have taken many courses on child development over the years and have enjoyed the opportunity to really learn why our children do what they do.

Our own children range in ages from six years old down to nine months old. With the exception of our baby, I have potty trained each one of our children in a weekend. After that, I shared my method with my brother and his wife, and they trained my niece and nephew in a weekend. Later, my friends used this method with success. Once I began blogging, complete strangers began to ask me about my potty training methods, then reported back to tell me that they have had success, as well.

As I tell my friends…

It is not the easy way to train,
but it is **fast and it is effective**.

Why Did I Write This Book?

Most of my friends have children close in age to my own children. When I potty trained ours so quickly, they began asking for advice and input. The word must have spread, because people that I didn't know started to e-mail me to ask me questions about potty training. I decided to write a short post on my method, and the comments starting coming in quickly! It then led to this information-packed eBook. I hope you find it helpful!

HOW OLD WERE OUR KIDS WHEN WE TRAINED THEM?

Our first son was 20 months old when he was potty trained. He was pee trained very early on, but it was several months before he would have a bowel movement on the potty or would stay dry during the night. I will dig into these topics later in this book.

Our second son was 22 months old when he was fully trained, pee and poop, in one day. He stayed dry all day long. He was never able to fully control his bladder at night, so night training has not yet been successful with him, and I do not push it.

Our second son was 22 months old when he was fully trained, pee and poop. He is dry almost every morning, but I still use a diaper on him at night, just in case. He regressed after our fourth baby was born. He was 26 months old when his baby sister was born and had accidents for over a week. I will talk about regression later in the book.

PROS AND CONS OF
EARLY POTTY TRAINING

● ● ●

PROS:

- I didn't want the mess of diapers.
- I wanted to eliminate the constant diaper bill. I stay home with our children, and a constant diaper expense can be a challenge to sustain. I talk about ways to save money in my other book, You Can be a Stay at Home Mom on One Income.
- I didn't want to have to change a three year old's dirty diaper.
- I wanted our children to feel independent, confident, and proud to wear their "big kid" underwear!
- It was just something that I wanted to do. It is not for everyone, but I personally wanted our kids trained early.

I do not judge parents that wait for their children to be trained. I don't even notice, to be honest.

Different strokes for different folks...

CONS:

- Our children were too young to dress themselves when I was training them, so I had to pull their pants on & off for them, which some might see as a bonus for waiting until your kids are a little older. I didn't mind this too much, but if you want to have an independent toilet trainer, you will want to wait.

It takes a lot of work and a lot of effort. Still, if you put that effort in during this one weekend, you will see the benefits in just a few days!

WHY DO I POTTY TRAIN THEM IN A WEEKEND?
What a lot of moms do, and something that I think is confusing to our kids, is to put their child in diapers or a pull-up, but tell them to use the potty instead of going in their diaper or pull-up. Isn't that confusing?

It would be like someone giving you a candy bar, but telling you to eat healthy. Or if someone gave you an electronic scooter but told you get a lot of exercise.

Which is it? Diapers or the toilet? This is why I do the "naked method" for 3 days. This is why it is successful. There are no gimmicks. It is not wishy-washy.

Consistency is key. "We go pee-pee and poop on the potty. We all do this and now you will, too. Yippee!"

The goal in our home (my own personal goal) was to have each of our children potty trained by the time that they turned two years old, and to do it in a weekend. Three days. (This is just the "main teaching" time frame. You will still remind them for weeks to come.) I liked our children to be trained by two years of age, because it makes life so much easier, and it can be done!

I am not one of those Moms who feels like they will get it when they are ready; I wanted them trained and in underwear. It was easier for me in the long run, and I knew that they could do it. So, they did!

CHILDREN RISE UP TO MEET OUR EXPECTATIONS.
It worked for us, and I hope that the same method works for you...whatever age you decide to give this a try!

2

Potty Training Around The World

How we train our children varies greatly based the country we live in.

It comes as no surprise that potty training in the United States is different from how potty training is handled in other countries. Let's take a look at the way that other countries potty train their children.

INDIA:

In India, they start to focus on training their babies around the 6-month age range. Their method makes a lot of sense to me, although I would never have the time to even attempt this.

They hold their babies above the latrine, and while they are doing this, they are making a hissing sound. The sound encourages them to go during these scheduled times. Most children in India are trained by 14 months old because they are praised for staying dry and reprimanded when they are soiled.

KENYA:

In Kenya, there is a tribal people group called the Digo tribe. They train their infants when they are just a few weeks old.

I have heard of this, but never attempted it myself. The reason is that there is almost always someone with the babies, so as soon as they notice the signs, they are taken outside and held over the ground. Are you ready for the best part? Most infants in this tribe (the Digo tribe) stay completely dry by 6 months of age, until they are given the opportunity to go outside! How great for them! I'm sure that some of you are wishing that you had done this, but it certainly isn't for me, and I am not going to teach you how to do this in Potty Train in a Weekend.

CHINA:

The same thing is true in China. A baby is trained at just a few months of age, and they stay dry all day, with frequent opportunities to go, by 6 months of age. To train their babies, the babies are held over the potty or over the ground.

Instead of hissing, as they did in India, the parents in China make a whistle sound, like the sound of urine. This signals the babies to go. When the children of China are a year old, they wear split-bottomed training pants, allowing the children to simply squat and urinate throughout the day. It is accepted that toddlers will relieve themselves wherever they are, even on sidewalks.

UNITED STATES:

In the United States of America, we tend to let our child lead the potty training more often than not. We use books, treats, stickers, charts, and rewards. Most children are trained around the age of three.

This thought process came about when a diaper company paid a pediatrician to recommend letting the child lead the potty training process, later in toddlerhood. Makers of diapers have increased their size of diapers to allow a child to stay in them longer.

GREAT BRITAIN:

Most parents in Great Britain do not complete training until their child is two years old. This has come about in recent years, as it used to be closer to 6 months.

GERMANY:

Germany is similar to the United States, allowing the children to remain in diapers until they are close to three years of age. The potty-training is child-led, and they let their child progress at their own pace with little interference.

3

Five Potty Training Methods

There are so many different Potty Training Methods! I have found, through friends and through doing research for this book, that there are more methods available than I know. I am going to explain the most popular choices that I have found.

METHOD 1:
INFANT POTTY TRAINING

As we see in other parts of the world, infant training can be done. It may be a little harder to do here in the United States, though, with our very busy lives.

We have long car trips, preschool, errands to run, work and much more. In my opinion, all of this makes training a baby hard. You have to be constantly watching your baby's expressions.

Ultimately, it may work for you, but it was not going to work for me. Infant potty training techniques can be very gentle and effective, if you choose to go this route.

METHOD 2:
THE CHILD-ORIENTED APPROACH
TO TOILET TRAINING

Pediatrician Dr. Brazelton started the idea of "child led" potty training. Proctor and Gamble hired him in the 1970s so that parents would keep their babies in diapers as long as possible. (The longer they are in diapers the more money they make.)

He was the practicing pediatrician that stated that, after observing an increase in toilet training failures, including toilet refusal which leads to constipation or behavior such as young kids smearing stool on walls and floors, we had stressed our children out.

Dr. Brazelton told the public that they were pushing their kids to be trained before they were ready, which caused the kids to do these things.

I believe that we are supposed to teach our children. If they are not ready, they may have a harder time learning, of course, but as we can see in other countries, even infants can learn to potty train; it may just take a little longer and a little more patience. The doctor's child-oriented approach is gradual and gentle.

This may be the perfect fit for you, if you don't mind waiting until your child tells you that he or she does not want to wear diapers anymore. I personally know a six year old (completely healthy and capable) girl that wears diapers. When I asked the parents why, they told me that they were waiting for her to tell them when she was ready. They choose to do child-led training.

METHOD 3:
FAST-TRACK POTTY TRAINING TECHNIQUES

Fast track potty training for toddlers was introduced in the early 1970s. This method teaches a child to use the potty before they are two years of age by using practice drills and pretend play, which is a great way to teach a child. An example of this is that the parent would place a doll or stuffed animal on the potty, urinating.

This method often offers rewards for success, as well as corrections for having an accident. The success rate for this method is high, if the parents follow instructions closely and stay consistent. We also train ours quickly and get it out of the way. Our children are confident on the potty, and we are happy with the great progress that they have made!

METHOD 4:
GRADUAL, PARENT-LED TOILET TRAINING

This approach is more laid-back, usually using a pull-up type of diaper. Parents are not pushing the potty, but asking their child if they would like to try.

They are offering rewards, but do not over-correct their child if an accident occurs. I think this method is probably the most popular of the methods, but also very time-consuming and drawn out. If you are reading this book, you are probably not looking for this type of method either.

METHOD 5:
BARE-BOTTOM METHOD
I personally combine this one with the fast-track method to make potty training a quick success in our home. This method is based on the idea that a child will not like being wet, so we let them learn to use the potty naked. It has worked for me... three times.

Combining several of these methods is how we get quick, successful results!

MY POTTY TRAINING METHOD EXPLAINED
I use the naked method of potty training and the fast-track method together. I leave our children completely naked. I do not put clothes on them except at rest time, or if we have to go somewhere, though I try to stay home during this process. I do not even put a shirt on them, because then I can't see when they are starting to pee.

If it is winter-time when you are potty training, you have a few options. You could use high socks or leg warmers. You could even do a tight pajama shirt that will still allow you to observe your child when they are starting to pee.

The key is to be able to see your child's private parts if you want to catch them when they start going. Bigger clothes will cover their private area, and you need to be able to tell when they are starting to go.

You will move to big-kid underwear on day three, but for the first two days, just keep them naked. They will probably love this! Our kids were thrilled with the fact that they didn't have to bother with clothes.

WHY I DO NOT USE PULL-UPS

I wanted our process to be quick, to the point, and done. I didn't want to drag it out with transitional diapers. Diapers work for many families, but I just used the naked method with each child and they were all trained very quickly.

4

Is Your Child Ready?

Start looking for readiness signs in your child from 16 months and up. I believe that each child has a window of opportunity when they are ready to be trained.

LOOK FOR THESE SIGNS WHEN YOUR CHILD IS 16-23 MONTHS

- Watching you (or bigger siblings) go to the bathroom
- Pretending to go to the bathroom or pretending to wipe
- Interested in body parts
- Having a dry diaper for more than an hour

Jump on board! If you miss this opportunity, it may be a while before this window is open again!

If you decide that your child is ready to use the potty, I am going to show you how to teach your child to use the potty in three days.

There isn't anything special about it - just consistency and a lot of time involved in the training (well, for those three days).

WHEN TO WAIT ON POTTY TRAINING

It is not wise to start training your child during a stressful time. Don't expect to see positive results if you begin when there are other things happening in the home.

EXAMPLES OF WHEN NOT TO START

- Family changes: new baby, new home, divorce
- When someone is sick
- New childcare: if you are going back to work or if your child will be starting to stay with someone else
- Excitement: don't start around a time when you will be planning a big birthday party or going on a vacation. You want to be able to be home and focused.
- When your child has a condition that may hinder potty training. If this is the case, talk to your doctor before training your child.

Before you read on, I want to tell you that the three day method is a lot of work. It is a lot of work because a lot of effort goes into those three days. Training your child early and in a short amount of time is wonderful, but not easy.

Just because it worked for me and many others does not mean that it will work for everyone (although I do think that it is possible and that you will have success!). With that being said, I think that it is completely worth all of the effort that you will put in during these three days!

5

Pick A Date And Make A Plan

B **E PREPARED!** This chapter is all about being prepared and it is VERY important. It can make or break your potty training success.

Before you officially begin the toilet-training process, get everything prepared. Pick a weekend or a three-day span where you have nowhere to be except home, potty-training your child. I do not go out during this time.

With our third son, I picked a week where my husband was off so that he could take the other kids where they needed to be while I stayed home to train our then 23 month old.

It is great to have an extra pair of eyes, if you can, to watch the other kids while you focus your attention on the potty trainer. If not, have some activities planned for your older children. You could rent a movie or game or get the kids a new toy.

I would just try to find something that is going to keep them as occupied as they can be. You could set up an activity or have activity stations (I have a lot of activities on my blog: yourmod-ernfamily.com)

WHY IS BEING PREPARED SO IMPORTANT?
I tried to potty train our third son at 18 months, and we failed. He was ready, but I was not prepared, so our potty training was not a success.

When I think back on why this first attempt did not work, I always land on these conclusions:

1. My husband was at work, and I had three very young kids at home by myself. This made it more difficult to focus on our 18 month old. (The second time around, I picked a week when my husband was off, and it worked like a charm!)
2. I had a hard time catching him when he would start to pee. I was not able to stay in one designated area of the home with the other kids home. I was not able to run him to the potty quickly enough because my focus was not solely on him.

   On the second day of potty training him, I stopped and decided to wait on his training until I could put my full at-tention onto him. I stopped training him and put him back in diapers (I felt that this was OK because it had only been one day. I would not suggest putting your child back into diapers after your child has potty trained, even if they re-gress; more on this later).

I decided to wait several more months, until my husband was able be home for a few days in a row to take care of our other children. Once we had a plan in place, we had success very quickly. He did regress when our fourth child was born, but I will tell you about that later in this book.

BE PREPARED AND BUY WHAT YOU NEED

Pick a potty chair and buy underwear before you begin potty training. There are many potty chairs (training toilets) to choose from. You may want to take your child with you to let him/her pick out a chair that they like. You may want to get one that your friend has recommended. Personally, I liked the Baby Bjorn chairs because they were small and our kids are very petite.

If you are training a young child, a smaller chair might be a better fit for you, as well. We also have one that looks like a frog. Our kids liked that one, too.

Another reason that I prefer the smaller chairs (instead of the insert that goes on top the big toilet seat), is because when your child has a bowel movement, they will use their feet to brace themselves to push down.

A child-sized potty chair that allows your child's feet touch the floor is a good choice. If you want to know how many you need, read on as we will discuss that strategy shortly.

BUYING UNDERWEAR

Buying big kid underwear is really fun for your child! Take your child with you and let him/her pick out special underwear. I have found that getting special big-kid underwear (their favorite character or TV show) makes a big difference in motivating them to not pee-pee in their underwear. You will want to buy more than one pack… you will need them. They may go through several each day. If our kids even get a DROP of pee in their underwear, they change them. This can be often during those first few weeks.

When you transition to underwear, having pants on during the first few days can be confusing and can cause accidents. I don't think that you should do pull-ups. They are just like diapers and make it difficult for your child to understand what is going on.

CLEANING SUPPLIES AND TOILETRIES

Next, you will want to make sure that you have all of your errands and running around done before you begin your three days of potty training. You will want to stay in the house as much as possible during your training period, so running out to get a loaf of bread is the last thing that you will want to do. Try to stock up on what you think you will need for a few days.

Another thing that you will want to have with you is cleaning supplies. If you need these when you are running your errands, pick them up. You will have accidents on your floor.

I kept our kids on all "hard surfaces" to make cleanup easier. Remember to have toilet paper and wipes near the potty when you start training!

Do all of your online things or phone calls ahead of time. Getting online for an hour is probably not going to work, because you will be keeping a very close eye on your child.

Save those tasks for nap time or bed time.

Enjoy this time playing with your child. They are getting 100% of your attention – what a gift for your relationship!

HOW MANY POTTY CHAIRS WILL YOU NEED?

You will want to decide how many you need at your house. I have several potty chairs and I have used them everywhere.

During those first few weeks (after the three day period), I moved our kid toilet to where we were. I thought that I would put them only in the bathroom, but that wasn't the case. It wasn't practical for me, as I stated on my blog, yourmodernfamily.com. You probably can tell that I am into practical things. Raising four kids would be hard to do if I didn't make things as simple and as practical as possible!

During mealtime, I would move the potty into the kitchen. I knew that it would take too much time to run to the bathroom, so for about two weeks, we had one in the kitchen. Yes, it is a little gross, but it worked.

I also had one little potty upstairs and one downstairs. It worked for us to have several at the beginning. You can borrow them from a friend of even buy one at a consignment sale for a couple of dollars. I bought ours new at the store because I knew that we wanted four children, so I would have more children to train. When we are not using them (after they have moved to the big toilet), they are stored under the sink, in the cabinet, until the next child is ready to be trained.

DECIDE ON A LOCATION

You will need to decide on an exact location. Think about the best place to do the potty training. You need to prepare the area. I block off an area of the house (a wide hallway, the kitchen, a back porch or deck if its not too hot or cold out).

Try to pick an area that is not carpeted, if possible. I put up a few gates and shut doors to keep our child and myself in that area. Will you be "camping out" during the days in the kitchen? The hallway? A screened in porch? If you have an ideal back yard, you could even train outside (if the weather is right - avoiding sunburns!). Just take your potty outdoors. I know friends that have done this.

Most importantly: Have your training potty in the area that you choose, ready to go. I stock our training area with toys, activities, snacks, and drinks.

Have a basket or several baskets that are full of toys, books, and cleaning supplies at the ready. I put our toilet on a towel because those first few days are hard for kids and they will be missing the potty. Having a towel under it will make the cleanup easier for you.

The goal is to play in that area all day, except naps and bedtime. You may want to eat meals at your normal place.

We have done both - had lunch in our area and dinner with the family at the table. If you decide to do your normal meal time routine, you should be persistent and take them to the potty before you sit down to eat and during your meal. Do whatever works for you.

If you do not want there to be an accident on your kitchen chairs, either eat in your area or put a towel under your child while they are eating. I usually did this around day two anyway, when I was ready for them to be eating with us, at the table, in their chairs.

6

Teach Them To Tell You

I t can be hard for a child to communicate that they have to go. They will not fully understand this for several weeks. It will be up to you to remind them! In order to prepare them for this, what you might want to consider doing is teaching them a sign for the potty.

For a week beforehand, every time that you go to the bathroom, you will want to say the word "potty" or "pee pee." Since your child is young and may not talk well just yet, pick a sign for potty (you can use the sign-language sign).

Signing can be easier for kids if they can't talk yet. None of my kids were talking well enough to tell me that they had to go when I was potty training them, so I taught all of them the sign. One of our children used it, the others learned the word "pee pee" relatively quickly when potty training, or just did the "pee pee dance" (holding themselves, or crossing their legs), which I knew meant "Hurry! Take me to the potty!"

7

Rewards

Rewards are important for reinforcing good use of the potty. When they have success and went on the potty I would make a HUGE scene! "Oh, Yeah, You did it! You pee-peed on the potty! You are awesome! You are amazing! You are such a big boy!"

Dance around, call your husband, call your Mom. (I did this with all of ours and the people on the phone were just as excited - or at least pretended to be!)

When my children peed on the floor, I would have an upset voice (not mean, just stern), and I would say, "No pee pee on the floor. Pee Pee goes in the potty."

The rewards that we offer include:

1. Praise
2. Flushing the potty. Our rule is that they can only flush IF they go to the bathroom.
3. Dancing around, hugs, kisses (Make it fun! Encourage them to go by really having fun with them when they go.)

I did not offer candy or stickers for pee-pee. You might want to offer rewards if you think that it will work better for your child. You know your child the best, so do what you think will work.

Praise was enough incentive for our kids. The others are great, but I didn't want to be giving a sticker or M&M for months and I didn't want them to associate praise with food (I didn't want them on a talk show for emotional eating issues in the future! Ha!).

I never did a chart of any sort. I didn't want to have to keep up with a chart. We don't really have any 'charts' in our house anyway. We have our chore basket and we have our cotton ball jar reward system, but we don't use charts because in the end, it is just something else on MY to-do list. (I have both of these systems on my blog, yourmodernfamily.com, if you are interested in learning more.)

Plus, our kids were only one at the time that I trained them to use the potty, so the chart idea was too "old" for them to understand.

As far as snacks for a reward, my brother and sister-in-law used Fruity Cheerios and fruit loops for a 'food reward.' I think that is a great idea if you want to use food as a reward, because it is a healthier option than candy.

Decide ahead of time which sort of rewards, if any, you are going to use, and be consistent with it. Your child will come to expect it and it will help this process be successful!

8

Fluid Intake When Training

During the three-day-training session, you probably want to increase their drinks. This will help give them more opportunities to go to the bathroom. If they are drinking a lot, you can count on them going to the bathroom at least once an hour, if not more. I find that juice and water go through them quicker than milk. I gave our kids a lot of water or diluted juice. I didn't give them any sugary drinks during this time.

Since they are in a smaller area, I didn't want them to have "sugar rushes" when I couldn't take them out to run around too often.

After the initial three day session is over, you may want to limit how often they are drinking. Of course you will want to give them enough fluids; just don't let them walk around the whole entire day with a sippy cup full of water unless you want to take them to the bathroom all the time. Stop all drinks after dinner to help with night-time wetting.

Do not let them have caffeine (tea and soda). This will cause accidents, at least early on in the training. My brother and sister-in-law gave both of their children a lot to drink when they were potty training them. Juice boxes and flavored water worked well because their kids normally don't drink a lot of those things, so they were excited to have it!

It really helped to encourage their kids to urinate more often, giving them more chances to use the potty. I didn't do this with our first son, but when I did it with our other kids, it made a difference.

I would encourage drinks. Just keep one out for them to grab when they want it. If you don't normally buy juice, this is a good time to buy it (we just dilute ours with water).

YOU ARE NOW READY FOR DAY ONE!

9

Day One

On the first day, start out by waking your child up (or waiting until they wake up) and taking your child to the potty as soon as he or she wakes up. They will probably have to go if you can catch them before they have had a chance to pee in their diaper. If not, don't worry about it and move on to your next step...20 minutes.

You will take your child to the bathroom often. Every 20 minutes (yes, every 20 minutes). Take them to your potty spot, place him on his training potty and say "Go pee," in a happy voice. Now, they will not be able to pee every twenty minutes. We are just teaching them to sit and try to go.

Hopefully, your child will be able to go every few times (maybe once an hour or once every two hours). This may not happen on the first day, but best-case scenario is that they are trying and pushing each time.

They should have gone at least once or twice by the end of the first day. Even a little trickle of pee is great progress! (We are helping them to avoid an accident by giving them a lot of chances to use the potty).

I didn't really praise too much for just sitting, but a simple, "Good try, buddy," every time they sit is helpful. I saved the praising for the real thing. I want them to be excited that I am excited. This will motivate them to use the potty.

Now onto the important part of this training method. When they start to pee on the floor (and they will!) you have to QUICKLY run over, scoop them up, and run them to the potty. When I would see them starting to pee on the floor, I would yell "Oh no!! No pee pee on the floor!! Pee pee goes in the potty!" as I was running them to the training potty.

I did this every time. This is the reason that you are restricting your space. You don't want to be on the other side of the house from the potty when this happens.

A few steps to the potty will make the training process so much easier. Why? If you are just a few steps away, when you run them to the potty, they will probably still be peeing when you get there. This leaves pee in the potty! You can praise them already! You will show them that they got to pee in the potty.

EXAMPLE: Five minutes after our first potty-attempt, our son starts to pee on the floor. I see this, because I am watching closely, and I say "Oh No! Pee-pee goes in the potty!" I swoop him up, take him four steps to the training potty and sit him down to finish. He finishes in the potty. Success. I cheer and smile. I take him off and show him all of that great pee in the potty. I hug him!

Now, we get to take the little insert out of the training potty, and carry the insert to the big potty together. (Yes, I let them help me. They loved it!) We dump the pee in and he flushes it. I say "Bye-Bye, Pee-Pee!"

We wash our hands and I hug him again, telling him I am so proud that he got pee-pee in the potty. We then go back to our designated area and see where he peed on the floor. I will say, "Oh, Yuck! Pee pee is on the floor." I actually point to the pee and say, "No pee on the floor. Yuck! Pee pee goes in the potty," and point to the potty. Clean it up, and repeat…for three days!

If they don't go again within 20 minutes, take them over to the potty and let them "try." Repeat every 20 minutes. Now that you have shown them what is going to happen, you need to keep it up every twenty minutes, all day long. Yes, this is exhausting. It pays off.

Remember to keep them naked all day (except at nap time and bed time). I put them back in a diaper for these times, when they are resting in their cribs and when I am not with them.

Consider it a success if your child attempts to run to the potty, pees on the potty, or says "Uh-oh" when they had pee running down their leg. This was the case for our kids, starting around the middle of day one.

Keep in mind that each child is different. Their personalities are different, and the rate and way that they potty train will be different.

Our oldest son was pretty much trained by the end of day one. Our second son needed a few more days of practice. Our third son did great, until we put him back into his underwear on day three (more on that later).

10

Day Two

Welcome to day two! On day one, they really don't understand the concept, but they will learn that pee pee does not go on the floor. Now, on day two, we will expand on that and help them grasp the concept.

By day two, our kids had pretty much stopped having accidents, and they were using the potty over 70% of the time. If your child is using the potty more than half of the time, I think that it is safe for you to move from taking them to the potty every 20 minutes, to taking them to the potty every 30-40 minutes.

If you feel that they would benefit from another day of 20 minutes, do it! It will only help your child, if you are up for the challenge again. Two days of every twenty minutes should be enough to really get the idea to sink in. If it's not working by day two (minimal accidents - maybe three per day?), you might want to hold off for a few more weeks. Or if you are feeling up to it, push forth and give it another day.

We are using the same idea for day two: take them to the potty often. Praising when they go on the potty and telling them that we do not go on the floor is important. You also want to stay in your "potty training area" if they are having a lot of accidents.

If they are using the potty on demand or not having many accidents, you can probably extend your area, just a bit. As long as you can still watch them, this can work. They will still be having some accidents, so keep that in mind when you decide (I never wanted to extend our area to our carpeted living room until they were not having many accidents).

I would still keep them in a diaper at naptime and during the night. Sleep potty training takes time, and I was just too exhausted during our first weekend. But it can be done. If you are feeling up to it, you can always do this now.

I have a chapter on how to night-train your child later in the book. Night-training was never on the top of my list, but it may be for you. Do what works for you and your child!

YOU ARE READY FOR DAY THREE!

11

Day Three

On day three, you can now move to every hour. (Still naked in the morning.) You will still want to keep them in a semi-contained area, such as one floor of your home if it is two stories, or close a few bedroom doors, if it is a ranch-style home or apartment. Keep them close, though you don't have to stay in the close quarters from before.

Continue to take your child to the bathroom every hour, or more often if needed. Your child should be using the potty and not having as many accidents by now, if you have been able to catch them every time. (You will miss a few... that's okay!)

Half way through the third day, when you feel relatively confident that they are getting the idea of using the potty, you can move them to underwear. This is going to be really hard for them. This is when I wanted to give up with each of our kids.

It feels like a diaper. It is confusing to them, so you have to stay ontop of it. You have to be extra careful and watch them closely. Look for signs (they will look at their legs if they pee in their underwear, say "Uh-oh!" or start to take them off) and respond to them quickly.

Your child will probably have an accident on this day; they will probably start to pee in their underwear. They may look sad or maybe they won't care at all, but you have to just stick to it. Do not give up! Our kids were fully trained by the end of the third day. If you can make it this far, you can finish the training. We had a struggle with underwear with our third child.

When I put underwear on him, he immediately started peeing in them. I think that he felt like it was a diaper. I had to go back to day one's process of taking him every 20 minutes (keeping him in underwear) in order to help him get used to it.

We did this for all of our third day, so I extended our main potty training one more day (it took us four days instead of our normal three). I use the phrase "main potty training" because you are never really done until they are independently using the potty, without your help, which is weeks or months away.

When your third day comes to a close, you still need to remember that you will be in the training stage for about a month. This just means that you need to remind them a little more often. They probably won't have accidents if you stay on top of it (taking them every hour or two. You will know how often your child goes, so just be sure to take them in intervals.)

I kept our kids naked at home as much as possible in the first few weeks, until I felt confident that they would not have any accidents.

If we were home, they were naked or in underwear all the time, for at least a month. I want you to know that it was months before our kids told me that they had to go without being reminded. They didn't have accidents during this time; they just held their pee until I took them. I took them every hour or every couple of hours, regardless of whether they were showing signs or not. This just about eliminates the accidents.

Try to remember that, if you have to go out (grocery store, to eat... wherever you are going), have your child go to the bathroom before you leave and then again when you get where you are going! You might want to take them more often, in order to avoid an accident outside of the home during those first few months. We never left home without our travel potty (our small Baby Bjorn potty).

If I didn't want to take them to the potty at our destination, I would have them go before we got out of the car, using our travel potty. Once, when I was at the pediatrician's office, another mom took her child to the bathroom three times during the hour that I was there.

They walked past our room every time, so I was able to hear him say "I peed!" when he would walk out of the bathroom. He was so proud of himself! I think she was in full potty-training mode. He was probably a newly turned two-year-old.

I'll talk more about potty training on the go later in the book, but the point is that they will go often, and that you need to continue to take them often, even if you are out.

HERE IS THE BIG REMINDER:

It is hard for them to tell you, so you have to watch for signs from them. Dancing, holding himself or herself, or trying to hide are all major signs.

Remember, they will most likely learn when they have to pee by first going a little bit on the floor or in their underwear, then realizing that pee is coming out.

Once they have seen you running them to the potty, they will learn that they need to be on the potty when this happens.

This is OK, and it is how they learn. They may start to acknowledge by saying "uh-oh." This how our first son told me every time.

Just stick to the plan. They aren't born knowing how to go on the potty, so we are training them. Just as you would train them to drink from a cup, write their names, or tie their shoes. We have to show them how to use the toilet.

12

Regression

cannot begin to tell you how many people tell me that their child was using the potty and then one day started having accidents. It is normally after the birth of a child or some sort of big event. No matter what the case, regression is common.

I try not to potty train our kids around a big event (baby being born, moving, etc.) so I trained each of them a month or two before the next baby was born. I will openly say that each of our children regressed when the new baby came anyway. It would have been wise of me to train them AFTER the baby was born, but I knew that I wouldn't have the time or energy to devote to that type of training (I was always exhausted from lack of sleep after each of our four children were born).

Having accidents again after being potty trained is completely normal.

My mom told me that my brother pulled down his pants and peed on the floor when they brought me home (he was almost three at that time). He had been fully potty trained for almost a year when I was born, and he still regressed.

It happened with our son, and it may happen with your child. Just be prepared with a plan.

HOW DO YOU HANDLE REGRESSION?
I went back to the weekend naked method, but a little more laid back. I would say that I did the "Day Two" again. I corrected them when they had an accident and said "No! No! We pee pee in the potty! Pee pee on the floor is yucky!" It took a couple of days to get them back on board, but they will come around.

Just stick to it. I didn't think that I would ever punish a child for having accidents, until our third son regressed. When our daughter was born, he started to pee in his pants… a lot. I was not happy about this. I went back to the day two training with him and did better, but he still peed.

Now, if I thought it was accidental, I would have been more patient with it, but I knew that it was for attention. He was peeing and just not even caring at all! I had to do time-outs for him, and it worked. I put him in time out for two minutes (He was two years old. The general rule of thumb is one minute per year. If your child is three, do three minutes).

Again: time out should ONLY be used if you know that this is a discipline problem and not just the occasional once-a-week accident. You don't want to punish something that they cannot control.

My biggest piece of advice when dealing with regression is to be consistent. This is the most important part of potty training. Hands down.

CONSISTENCY.
<u>Do not go back to diapers, if you can at all help it.</u>

Remember to use a lot of positive reinforcement. You want to cheer and dance and give high fives for potty successes! If you can make it a positive thing and reward them with attention for using the potty, they will want to go. I found that when I did more praising, like I had done at the beginning, it really motivated him to go on the potty again. He was getting just what he wanted attention - but this time it was for making the right choice.

13

Boys: Sit Or Stand?

I have taught all three of our boys to urinate sitting down. When they are tall enough to reach the REAL potty (or use a stool), around three years of age, I transition them from sitting to standing. They are happy to stand ("like Daddy"), and if they would have wanted to stand earlier, I would be OK with it.

My rule is that potty training boys DO NOT hold their penis when they are peeing! Why don't I want them to hold it? This causes them to "aim," but they are not good at aiming yet, so they pee on walls. On the other hand, my grandma put cheerios in the toilet and had them hit the cheerios. That might work for you, if you are teaching them to aim.

I have found that it is just easier to let them stand there. If they just stand there, it naturally just flows into the big toilet. Remember: do not let them stand over the training potty. It will make a huge mess! If you want them to stand, let them use a small stool and stand over the big toilet.

A reader of my blog posted this comment in response to one of my posts: "About sitting vs. standing...I am a preschool teacher, and I have encountered MANY boys who are trained to pee in the toilet but still poop in their pants or hold it to the point where they have to visit the doctor. If they learn to sit and go pee, sitting to go poop feels natural. So I would make these 4 and 5 year old boys sit every time they went pee. This worked with all but 1 child… and he was a special case."

14

They Won't Poop On The Potty

What if they will pee but not poop on the potty? Once you have trained your child in three days, you might run into just a few potty training hurdles. This is the biggest concern that my friends and I hear: "They will pee on the potty, but not poop."

I went through this with our son and hear it SO often from other moms! When I was dealing with this with our son, I had heard the story about a seven-year-old child waiting until he came home from school to put on a diaper to poop. I was so afraid this would be our son. (At the time, our child that was having problems with this was only 20 months old, but I still worried, like moms do.) He did get it a few months later. Once he got over the fear of going, he was fine and was able to use the potty consistently.

Why won't they poop on the potty? They are scared. They literally think that a part of them is falling off. I know that sounds ridiculous, but every doctor that I asked has given me this same answer. I have even heard of showing your child a kid's anatomy book to explain that the food goes in and comes out.

One idea was to feed them corn so they could see it in the potty. This is gross, but it makes complete sense. It shows them that it is not a part of their body.

Another reason that your child may be resisting pooping on the potty is if your child has waited to have a bowel movement.

When they finally decide to go, it can be painful. One painful experience can be remembered for quite some time, hindering the urge to want to try it again. You should talk to your doctor about some easy solutions (oils, foods, and drinks that you can give to him or her) to make having a bowel movement less painful. You do not want your child to become constipated.

My friend's daughter started taking Miralax, and it really helped her. (Ask a doctor before giving your child anything!) Our one son was trained to pee on the potty at twenty months, but it wasn't until he was almost 24 months that he learned to poop on the potty. Our other boys were pee and poop trained during the three-day session. It just depends on your child.

So how did I get them to go poop on the potty? I will give you as many tips as I can for this common issue!

One method that I used for this (its a little weird): putting our son on his little potty, over a towel, in front of the TV. He liked watching Sesame Street at the time, so I just moved it in front of the TV.

He could just sit there, naked, and watch his show. He had a lot of time to let the bowel movement happen, without a lot of pressure. If he got up, I just turned the show off until he was ready to try it again later. He liked this, because it was certainly a treat to have the potty in the living room!

With our oldest son, I even let him eat an ice cream cone on the potty when having him poop on the potty. I am not above bribery when it comes to this. I just wanted it done, and you know what? If bribery with food helped in this one occasion, so be it.

I don't normally offer food as a reward because I don't want our kids to have food struggles later in life, but this one week when they are one year old is not going to make that big of an impact in their lives or relationship with food.

In the end, what ended up working for us was, when I knew he had to poop (all of our kids went early in the morning), I put him on the potty with a lollipop, in front of the TV, so he would just sit there for about 15 minutes eating it. If he got up, I took the lollipop away. He cried the first few times that I took it away, until he realized that he could have it if he sat there.

Do not give into their crying for the lollipop if they get up. I knew that eventually he would have a bowel movement. I didn't force him to sit on the potty, but that was the only way that he was going to get his treat, so he stayed.

If you are keeping the potty in the bathroom, I noticed that if I sat in there and talked to him (to distract him from being afraid, which is why they won't poop on the potty), he would forget and go. You could play a little movie for them on your phone or tablet. You could read a book or sing songs.

Keeping them distracted from the fear of going will help them to poop on the potty.

Rewarding was huge in our house for pooping on the potty. I really rewarded for this. You could buy some special prizes or print out coloring pages from a favorite TV show or make special cookies. These rewards are only if you are having major struggles with one issue and you need some extra incentive to help them.

In our home, they only got the special treat for going poop on the potty. Once they get it the first time, it should be much easier. Occasionally, they will regress with pooping. Don't give up. Go back to the naked method for a few days and keep working at it!

At some point, your child may get a stomach bug, and you will probably want to get pull-ups for this. If they are having diarrhea, it changes things. Don't tell them that it is a diaper; just tell them that you bought them new "special underwear" to wear while they are sick. If they have been potty trained for a few months, you won't have to do this. They will be able to understand when they have to run to the bathroom.

Our first son got sick a week after potty training, at my parent's house. I had to revert to diapers for a few days until he was better. When he got better, we just went back to one day of potty training and he was right back on the potty-trained-wagon. If this doesn't work, don't give up. I promise that, eventually, he will go.

You poop on the potty, right? **Your child will, too.**

Give it time and keep trying. Try first thing in the morning. If you are worried that they are completely avoiding pooping, just to avoid going on the potty, let them have a diaper at nap time and at bedtime. They will go in their diaper. (I didn't want our kids to get constipated over the fear of having an accident, so if they pooped at nap time, so be it. I just kept trying when they got up). They all pooped on the potty by two years of age. It will happen, so don't worry!

15

What To Do With Accidents

How do you deal when your child poops in his or her pants?

I just kept telling him "No! No!" when he would poop in his pants. It was gross, and I would let him know that I did NOT approve! To clean up, I would take the dirty underwear & dump the poop in the potty (while he watched) and we would flush it.

I would then take the soiled underwear to the laundry room and put them into the washer, with him watching me. The whole time, I was visibly acting like it was yucky and that I didn't approve. I had an upset (not mean, just upset) expression on my face.

Remember to take the phase that they are going through with a grain of salt and tell yourself that "This, too, shall pass." If you suspect that your child is having a medical condition that interferes with potty training, you should resolve it before pushing the issue.

16

Potty Training On The Go

t is wise to buy a travel potty! They are cheap and you can keep one in your car. I like the Baby Bjorn travel potty. It is tiny and portable. Speaking of the car, you will want to be sure that you have an extra set of clothes and disinfecting wipes in your car at all times.

Accidents are called accidents for a reason.

They come at times when we least expect them, and they can make a mess. I still keep an extra set of clothes in a bag in the trunk of our car for each child, although I often forget to replace them when we get home.

AVOID A MESS IN THE CAR

First things first, have them try to pee before you leave the house! In those first few days, if we went anywhere and I didn't think they could hold it, I would put them in underwear and put a diaper over the underwear.

Why both? I used the underwear because I wanted them to feel when they were wet, but I used the diaper on top to keep the car seat clean. Now that our boys are older and I am not training them anymore, I can just keep a throw-away water bottle in the car.

When I finish up a bottle of water, I just keep the bottle in the car. If we are out and they have a true "potty emergency" and can't wait until we get home, they can urinate in the bottle and I can just throw the whole thing out and replace it with a clean bottle when we get home. You are probably thinking that this is pretty gross, I know - but, well, this is "potty talk" after all!

A travel potty works really well for these emergencies, too. They are easy to clean (just dump it outside and use a wipe to clean it out), and I keep grocery bags in my glove compartment so I can throw old wipes in there or clothes that have being soiled. I keep at least three grocery bags in my car at all times for roadside potty breaks and emergency clean up.

17

Potty Training At Night

Let's talk about bed-wetting and night training. First, just know that some kids are not capable of this until they are older. Our first son was trained to stay dry at night when he was a year old. Our second son is four and still has accidents at night. I will tell you HOW to train them, but as our doctor has told us, if their body is not physically ready to wake them at night or to hold the urge to urinate for 12 hours, there is nothing that you can do about it.

If they are still having frequent accidents at seven years of age, you will want to bring it to your doctor's attention. Our child's pediatrician said that she does not raise a red flag until they are eight years old. I will tell you how I night-train our kids, but again, we have one child that is just not physically ready. There is nothing that we can do about it.

With that being said, here is what worked with our other children, and how we could tell they were ready.

Are they ready for night---training?

Do they wake up with a dry or almost dry diaper? You will have to have them out of the crib to night train them because they need to be able to get in and out of their bed on their own. If you have stairs, be sure to have a gate guarding the stairs.

I would certainly not get them into a big-kid bed for this reason, as potty training at night can wait (one transition at a time). I loved when our kids were in their cribs. I slept better at night knowing that they were safe in their cribs and couldn't get out.

We had our kids in big-boy beds early because we always needed the crib for the new baby, but I didn't rest as easily. In order to train our kids at night, I put their training potty in their room, on a few towels. (The towels are to protect your floors in case of an accident). The potty chair that we kept on our second story would go into their rooms at night and back into the bathroom in the morning.

What did we do every night before they went to sleep?

Every night, I put them in a diaper, turned out the lights, and we practiced our "going potty at night routine" several times. I helped them for the practice round.

They would:

1. Walk to the potty in their room.
2. Pull down their diaper (I don't buy pull-ups; I just made their diapers loose enough to pull on and off)
3. Sit on the potty.

4. Try to go pee.
5. Stand back up.
6. Pull their diaper back up (I left them in only a diaper and a shirt to train at night because pajama bottoms just add extra hurdles)
7. Get back into bed.
8. Lay down.

We practiced this about half a dozen times the first night and at least two times a night (before bed) for a week, until they got the hang of it completely. They thought that the practicing part was great! Turn out the lights and just use their nightlight when practicing what they will do, just like at bedtime.

You want it to be as much as the real thing as possible. I did this because I did not want them to wake me up all night long to use the bathroom. I also was nervous about them being in the bathroom with all of the water (sink, toilet) without me. This was a safe way to help them train at night.

Tell them that YOU will empty the potty in the morning to avoid a huge mess!

When our children turned three, I stopped keeping a potty in their room and taught them to use the bathroom instead. (Put a gate on the steps to be sure that they don't fall down on accident when walking to the bathroom.)

Keep a night light in the bathroom and in the hall. You will probably hear them anyway, because I think that we, as parents or caregivers, are light sleepers. But let them try to be independent. Just listen, but don't get up to help unless they need it.

My brother and my sister-in-law had a bathroom right next to their child's bedroom, so they just had him use the bathroom at night when he was trained, around two years of age. He never had an issue with this and trained himself at night.

At first, he would call to them for help, waking them up to tell them that he had to go pee. After a few nights of being dry, they were able to just leave his diaper off, and he started taking himself to the potty without needing help.

Something that helped all of our children was to take them before YOU go to bed. We take our kids to the bathroom before getting into bed every night (the kids who still have accidents).

Around 11:00 or midnight, I pick them up, take them into the bathroom, put them on the potty and tell them to "go pee." I then take them back to bed. They never remember the next day, and it always helps to prevent accidents. If they have had a lot to drink, you will want to make sure that you remember to do this, even if they had been staying dry. This works for so many parents!

If kids have any caffeine, then bed-wetting is more likely to happen. Also, remind them to go first thing in the morning! If they have a diaper on, take it off right away. You don't want them sitting around in a diaper for thirty minutes when they have had a long night of staying dry. They will go in their diaper if you provide the opportunity.

Another tip is to stop drinks a few hours before bed. My friend gave me this tip when our first son was potty training. It never dawned on me, but it worked that very first night. If our kids are thirsty, they can have milk. I have found that drinking water causes accidents for our children, if it is close to bedtime. I stop all drinks, except milk, after dinner.

For some reason, milk doesn't seem to be a problem. You can also leave them in a diaper at night. If they are ready to be dry all night long, they will be dry in their diaper or in their underwear. If I think they might have an accident, I leave them in a diaper. If it is dry in the morning, I make a big deal about it with a lot of praise!

If you have an older child (five years or older) still having accidents at night, I have another suggestion. This next tip came from my friend's pediatrician.

On top of the suggestions listed above, you will want to wake your child before you go to bed, but this time you are not going to help them at all. You are going to wake them up. They will then get out of bed. They will walk to the bathroom. They will pull down their pants, use the bathroom, flush the toilet, pull their pants up. They will wash their own hands.

They will walk themselves back to bed. You give them a goodnight hug and kiss and head to bed. With this strategy, you are teaching their body to learn the signs and to wake from them. It can take six to eight weeks before you see success.

So be patient.

18

Potty Training With Special Needs

Potty training a child with special needs can be a little more challenging, but that is not to say that it can't be done. The average age to potty train a child with special needs is much higher (averaging around age four or five), so don't feel defeated or discouraged if your neighbor's two year old is potty trained while you are working on training your four year old. Your child is unique, just like we are all unique, and we need to do what works for each child.

I want to start this chapter by telling you that we do not have a child with special needs (although if you have ever read my blog, you know how we were very close, when our son was born hypertonic). What I will say is that I am a play therapist, and I work with children with developmental delays on a daily basis.

The 102 children that I work with are very young, so I have been able to help many families with the issue of potty training their child, and I have seen success.

While no parents want to push a child with special needs to do what he or she cannot do, if you can help them to be able to use the toilet, the difference in the level of self-esteem in your child will be amazing. It is such an accomplishment for your child, and they will feel proud, as they should!

Before beginning the training, I would have a quick chat with your pediatrician, any therapists, and any specialists that you and your child see. They will give you advice that is very specific to your child. This is important, and I would not skip this step. I would also have a physical done before going forward, to be sure that there is nothing that will make it harder for your child (such as a urinary tract infection).

So... Are you ready to go?

First, you are going to want to watch for signs. You need to see the same signs of readiness that I wrote about earlier in the book. (Are they staying dry for at least an hour at a time? Are they showing signs before having a bowel movement? Does he or she seem interested in the bathroom or in you when you go to the bathroom?)

If your child seems to be hesitant or resistant, you will want to wait. This is especially true in this unique situation. Don't worry about it - just pick back up in about two months or as soon as you see their interest pique.

If you think that he is ready to go, just prepare him for what is going to happen. They will start using the bathroom, they will flush the loud toilet, they will wash their hands with warm water, they will wear underwear with their favorite things on it, etc.

Things to remember before you jump right in:

1. It is okay that your child might be older. This is his/her time.
2. The process may take longer – a weekend probably won't cut it. That is OK.
3. You will have to do more (help with clothing, help with the toilet, help with washing hands).
4. **Accidents WILL happen**! Be prepared, both emotionally with expectations and physically prepared with some cleaning products!
5. Your family should be prepared. You may need a break or some help or even just someone to listen. Tell them what you are doing. Their support will be very important.
6. You can do this, as a team. Look at all that you have done together so far.
7. Every child is different and advice that will work on one child may not work on another. That is just fine, because you will learn what works with your child.

TYPES OF DELAYS AND HOW
TO APPROACH POTTY TRAINING

Physical Delays

Physical delays can make it harder to train a child. I have had to offer suggestions to parents such as installing bars next to the toilet for the child to use for stability or offering a stole for the child's feet.

Remember to plan out ideas for what will need to be done when your child has to go – will you be helping? Will they need your assistance forever? Will they be able to go if you have a special area prepared for them (such as, perhaps, the support bars?)

Visual Disabilities

Visual disabilities can make it much harder for children beginning to potty train. They are not able to observe other children using the bathroom. They cannot see how you walk to the toilet, how you reach over to flush the potty, how you turn on the water and check the temperature to wash your hands. You will need to tell them.

They will be relying on their other senses: smell, sound and touch. Children with visual delays may have a harder time in the beginning.

It will be important to leave the training toilet in one place and not move it, except to clean it. You will need to show them how to determine how much toilet paper to use, how to sit on the potty each time, what to do afterwards, how to find the sink and soap, etc.

A few tips to help:

- Keep the bathroom smelling clean (smell is huge here!)
- Let your child explore the bathroom AFTER you have cleaned it, to make it a good experience and encourage your child to want to be in there.
- Use hand-over-hand to show your child where things are (let them place their hand under yours as you explore the bathroom: toilet, handle, door, water).

Hearing Impairments

Children who are hearing impaired may have a hard time if communication is difficult or if they cannot call out to tell you that they need help. When our daughter had been trained for several months, she would alert us that she needed to go to the bathroom because she would start yelling "Mommy! My pee! My pee!" (her words for "I need to go pee!")

Remember to pay close attention and communicate well with your child, adapting the method to your style of communication with each other.

A few tips to help:

- Let your child watch you use the bathroom.
- Look through books about toilet training and learn appropriate sign language.

- Use the same sign each time.

Remember that being audibly verbal does not have to stop you. My children were not talking when I taught them to use the bathroom, either, since they were too young.

Cerebral Palsy

Children with cerebral palsy have a harder time with toilet training because their bladder awareness and control begin much later. I worked with a child with Cerebral Palsy for several years, and when he was learning to use the potty, he would become VERY fidgety before going. He was almost three years old, so it was obvious to us, and it gave us a great sign that told us "I need to go right now!"

His other challenge was staying on the potty. We found that we needed to use a training potty with handles on the sides and a higher back. It was very helpful! His mother also told me that it was helpful when mom would sit on the potty and hold her child in front of her, on the potty. This offered a physical support while her child was going and allowed him to use the regular toilet and not the training toilet once he turned three.

Behavioral Disorders (Autism, ODD, ADHD, FAS, Sensory)

On my Facebook group, I encourage reader questions and answers (and the shared answers are always amazing!). This is one of the questions that I get more than any other about potty training: "How do you potty train a child with autism or sensory disorders?"

This is one of the more challenging obstacles, because you know that your child is physically capable of doing this, but the disorder is stopping them. You will really need to know your child and what motivates them to succeed.

These children are often very motivated by praise. You could even offer a small reward (such as a sticker) for doing a good job and trying to use the potty without becoming frustrated. I normally don't use charts or rewards, but this situation is unique, and anything goes.

Another thing to remember is that you are changing their routine, so they are going to have to adjust to this new routine (ex: taking off clothing, using the bathroom where they have not spent any time, etc.).

Still, nearly all children with behavioral disorders can be toilet trained, even if it takes longer (sometimes, up to a year).

A FEW TIPS TO REMEMBER:

- Have your child examined by a pediatrician (he/she is at a higher risk of constipation and loose stools)
- Observe your child's patterns to see if he has trouble with certain things: maybe the floor is too cold and you need to have slippers by the bathroom door. Maybe the smell is off-putting and you need to switch the bathroom cleaner that you are using? Maybe the toilet is too loud for your child and you will have to flush it for him/her when they leave the room?

- Observe the times that your child needs to go (look for signs like stopping/pausing). How long after eating or drinking does it normally take before he urinates or defecates? Do certain foods or drinks make it work (for our kids, caffeine was a HUGE no-no during toilet training!)
- Explain everything. Then explain it again. Use charts that show what is going to happen (first, next, then, last)
- If your child is hesitant to go to the bathroom, offer rewards.
- Don't be angry, but instead, try to just be consistent. "No pee in pants!" You just want to continue taking your child to the potty- they will learn that they go several times a day so that it becomes a routine.

Overall, just remember that this will be a learning curve for both of you. Consider letting them watch videos about it (there are some appropriate potty training videos on YouTube) and reading them books, as well.

Remember that you don't want to panic if they have an accident and you don't want to rush this process. This is very different from how you would potty train a child without a delay, but remember that it is okay to go at your own pace (and their own pace).

Work on maintaining your patience and not becoming frustrated, because that can be felt by the child. Be sure to also give your child immediate feedback. I know that we expect things to happen a certain way and that is where the frustration comes in, but try to remain calm about it. "Don't sweat the small stuff," as I remind my husband every day.

Potty training your child is important, but <u>don't feel defeated</u> by it if it doesn't go your way.

19

Tips From Other Parents

If this is going to be the most helpful and valuable potty training book, it needs more than me. I would need to get tips from other parents about potty training children.

Every child is different, and I hope that these tips will help you when you find what works for you. You know your your child more than anyone.

Stick with the main plan, but navigate your own path to make it fit for your family and your child!

TIPS FROM OTHER PARENTS:
"Start young. I have trained three boys and I have started young each time. My reasons for training our kids at a young age included helping them not have to sit in soiled pants, keeping us from changing dirty diapers, saving money on diapers, and helping them become aware of eliminations. I think there's a definite "plus" when you start early. It gives you a chance to begin before they have a chance to become defiant, minimizing the power struggles with you about it.

I start at 18 months. People will think you're crazy, but globally, more than half of kids potty train around that time... so it is not crazy at all! Another tip would be to dedicate a whole week to it (if they are pretty young) and just be on the floor with them.

I thought this was going to be horrible, but at the end of the week, after I got peed on too many times to count, I just loved the time that we had spent together. I loved seeing him learn something new, becoming proud of himself, and just playing and enjoying my baby with no other agenda than watching and studying them. It was a special time that I wasn't expecting!

There's nothing to be afraid of! Countless moms are always scared or dreading the start of it, but really, it's what you make of it. I already told Brandon that I want to train my grand-babies one day, too! I love to see that "aha!" moment in their face when it clicks."

~ Christina P.

"A struggle would be pooping in the potty. My first two struggled so much with this. They would cry and get scared, but I just held them, loved on them and held their hand the whole time.

They pooped on the potty kicking and screaming the first time, and then after they saw what they did, they were so proud of themselves that they quickly got over it. I never did do the transitional poop in diaper, then make a hole in diaper thing. That is one way that parents have of transitioning their kids to poop ... I'm more of a "get over it" kind of person and know it just takes one hit in the potty to start breaking that fear."

~ Pricilla

"I talked to his our son's pediatrician about potty training issues with stubbornness in the child. The pediatrician said, 'Every child is different. Keep trying until you find what works for him. Don't worry, mom, all kids are potty trained by the time they leave for college.'"

~ Christian

"With my kids, I would sit them on the potty when they get up in the morning and after naps also after meals. Let them sit there with their favorite toy or book. I have found they do better without me in the bathroom, and they call for me when done."

~ Sandy

"My middle son was stubborn when it came to #2 on the potty - absolutely refused, no matter the reward. So I finally told him that when we flush, the poop goes out to the sea to feed the fish - so if he didn't go, then the poor little fish wouldn't have anything to eat. My son, being the compassionate, sensitive little do-gooder he is, felt it was his mission to poop to "save" the fish. (After all, Nemo and Dory were counting on him!)"

~Liane

"No pull ups once you start!"

~ Abbey

"I have my kids drink lots of fluids... A LOT! That way I get a lot of training opportunities. We stay home, and once we start... it's no more diapers."

~ Liz

"Start early by putting them on the potty first thing in the morning as soon as they wake up (around 1 year). Usually, they naturally have to go pee. Also, have them go right before bath time when you undress them put them on the potty. Once you have done this, start introducing some diaper free time and putting on underwear.

Set a timer and take them to the potty every 20 minutes. When they first start wearing underwear, it's more of you being trained to notice signs they have to go and to catch them before they do it.

Lots of praise and excitement when they do go. When you get to the point to start venturing out of the house, take them to the potty first thing when you get in the store/restaurant and take them again before you leave.

~ Cheryl

"Two words: Mini M&Ms! Promise that each time your kid goes potty, she gets two or three; if she wipes herself (a huge challenge for us) then she gets four or five. This makes a big difference since I think one of the reasons kids don't like to go is because the business of learning to wipe is kind of yucky."

~ Donna

"I wholeheartedly recommend bribery as potty training motivation: We kept a small plastic piggy bank in the bathroom and rewarded every success (one penny for pee, two for poop). Our daughter was entranced - she would shake the piggy with a gleam in her eye and remark how heavy it was getting. When she was all done, we took her potty windfall and turned it into quarters to spend on rides at the mall."

~ Lisa

"Getting my son to learn the standing-up thing was hard, so we turned it into a game. I put five Cheerios in the potty and told him to aim at them when he peed. Every time he did it right, he got to pick out a prize from a bag of goodies I picked up at the dollar store."

~ Erika

"You can even make a chart to put stickers on when they are successful. I was using M&Ms as a treat for successful pottying, which works... BUT, there are two things wrong with that. First, she caught on pretty quick and started making me take her to the potty when she didn't need to go, in order to earn candy. Secondly, this teaches her that candy is a reward, which could cause some unhealthy food issues later on in life."

~ Elle

"I've heard all the tricks - stickers, bribing with toys, special underpants. But you have to pick something that's consistent with your parenting style. I didn't use rewards elsewhere, so I didn't want to start here. What did work: Lots of undivided attention, positive reinforcement, love, affection and pride when my kids were successful. Making a big deal about small steps of progress is key."

~ Diana

"We found that our son simply was not interested in remembering to go on his own, so we found the Potty Watch, which he loved. You program this wrist watch to play songs and light up at 30-, 60-, or 90-minute intervals; then it resets itself and starts the countdown all over again."

~ Heather

"My son mastered peeing on the potty pretty quickly, but nailing #2 took some extra effort. At first we had to watch for his "cues" to tell he was trying to go poop and then bring him to the bathroom. Because it took a while (sometimes more than a half-hour) we started reading to him to make the wait more fun. But above all else, patience, patience, patience is the key!"

~ Karen

"So I put the potty chair in the living room in front of the coffee table and put a jar of M&Ms on the coffee table. She loves M&Ms. I told her she could have an M&M when she used the potty chair. She wanted to sit on it all the time, so I didn't even have to put her on it. She wanted her M&M, so I told her "no pee pee, no candy." When she did go, I would give her just 2 M&Ms and she was happy.

On day two, I only put about 8 M&Ms in the bowl and tell her that, when they were gone, there was no more. She never asked for M&Ms after that. She would just tell me when she had to go. Now, this did not work for my son since he did not care about getting candy."

~ Betty

That is all there is! Remember, when it comes to potty training, "This too shall pass." Whatever the struggle is that you are having right now, be consistent and patient, and your child will soon get it! It is a lot of hard work for three days and a lot of reminders afterward, but the freedom from diapers and the confidence in your child are worth it. It can be done if you are ready for the challenge.

Ready, set, go!
Becky Mansfield

www.yourmodernfamily.com
www.beckymansfield.com

Find Me Online:
www.facebook.com/YourModernFamily
www.pinterest.com/BeckyMans
@YourModernFam

Check Out My Other Books...

Freed
from
Clutter

Organizing Room by Room

By Becky Mansfield

YOU CAN BE A STAY AT HOME MOM ON ONE INCOME

money saving tips

BECKY MANSFIELD

Notes:

Notes:

Made in the USA
Middletown, DE
28 January 2018